Color & Character:

a Contemplation of the Four Divine Qualities

by F. H. Robison

This booklet is a compilation of articles
that were originally published in
THE GOLDEN AGE
magazine
between February 4, 1920 and April 27, 1921
under the title **COLOR & CHARACTER**.

Minor typographic and spelling errors
that were in the original articles have been corrected.
These changes have not affected the meaning of what was written.

The cover diagrams are colorized renderings of some of the original
black and white illustrations which accompanied the articles.
The black and white illustrations appear within
in approximately the same place as
in the original columns.

ISBN 978-1-4116-8775-2

Printing/Distribution provided by:
Lulu Enterprises, Inc.
3131 RDU Center Dr., Ste. 210
Morrisville, NC 27560
www.lulu.com

SECTION	ORIGINALLY APPEARED	PAGE IN THIS EDITION
The Primary Colors	February 4, 1920	1
The Secondary Colors	February 18, 1920	3
The Tertiary Colors	March 3, 1920	5
Color Quality and Quantity	March 17, 1920	6
Chromo-Phono-Geometric Co-ordinates	April 14, 1920	11
Diphthongs and Triphthongs in Color	April 28, 1920	13
Color and Tone Pitch	May 12, 1920	15
Color and the Compass	May 26, 1920	17

[note: June through September 1920 THE GOLDEN AGE was published in a shortened version due to a shortage of printing paper, and the series did not appear during that time.]

Color and the Elements	October 13, 1920	20
Color and Temperament	October 27, 1920	22
Color and Its Maker	November 10, 1920	27
Color and the Messiah	November 24, 1920	31
Heart, Mind, Soul, Strength	December 8, 1920	34
Color and the Fine Arts	December 22, 1920	37
Color and Physiognomy	January 19, 1921	40
Color and Sex	February 2, 1921	43
The Cains and Abels	February 16, 1921	45
Color and World Empire	March 2, 1921	49
Faith, Hope, Love	March 16, 1921	52
Diagrammatic Summary	April 13, 1921	55

The Primary Colors

THERE is no need here of going into elaborate scientific discussions as to what the primary colors are (discussions, in fact, as to whether there be any primary colors at all), for in light analysis it seems to be very well established that red, green and blue-violet occupy such a position. But when we come to the realm of pigments for painting, drawing, dyeing and printing we have a different problem; and here, for all practical purposes, yellow, red and blue are primary. Black is not, strictly speaking, a color, but the presence of all three—none of them being reflected from the sunlight which strikes a black object or texture. The primary colors are elemental; they cannot be produced by mixtures.

Yellow is the most brilliant color, in brightness being nearest to the light of the sun. It is cheerful in its effect on the mind, sunny, buoyant, hopeful, jocund. Yellow has life-giving radiance and power to dispel gloom, as daffodils, buttercups, and dandelions seem to chase away the blue of winter.

Red is the warmest color and imparts the feeling of vitality, action, courage, and aggression. Red stimulates the nervous system, even the nervous system of a gobler or a bull. It is because of this forced stimulation and call to action that some sensitive people are temperamentally opposed to red. They are already too active, perhaps, and red comes to them like an angry challenge. Red associates itself with the thought of fire and must be as carefully handled and restricted or it will destroy as well as warm. Nature uses brilliant red but sparingly and then only where there are great masses of green to counter-balance it. All colors which contain red are warm in proportion to its presence.

Blue is cold, quiet and reserved. It is present in all shadows and never enthuses one to action, being in this respect a balance for yellow and red. Blue flowers are all modest and retiring, as the fringed gentian, the forget-me-not, etc. The restraint and formality of blue make it particularly suggestive of dignity.

Whoever understands color understands a universal language, like music. True, one may enjoy both tone and color and not understand either; but it is like hearing an opera in an unknown tongue—it leaves much to be desired.

Yellow advances; red in some hues remains about stationary, but in pure value tends to recede; blue recedes decidedly. Thus we have the foreground, the middleground and distance. There are no pure yellows in a middleground or distance and blue always predominates in the latter.

The Secondary Colors

THE combination of any two primaries forms a secondary or binary color. A secondary partakes of the interest and nature attaching to both its parents. For instance, green is much more interesting than either of its constituents, yellow and blue. Violet is more pleasing than either red or blue, and orange will hold the attention longer than either yellow or red.

When yellow and red are combined we have a fusion of the ideas of light and warmth, of cheer and action. The result is splendor in the realms of objects, or vivacity in the domain of conduct. Orange has great decorative quality, as seen in a bed of nasturtiums. Its complement is blue. Too much orange is toned down by the presence of quantities of blue. Gold (which is orange in color) shows to best advantage in small quantities on garments of blue.

Red and blue combined form violet—the deepest color on the scale. It is the child of vitality and dignity, and its nature is therefore one of serenity, majesty. In its tints, such as lavender and lilac, it becomes distinctly feminine in delicacy and refinement. Its complement is yellow.

Blue and yellow give us green. It is more cheerful than blue and has more repose than yellow. It may, therefore, be called restful. Heaven has graciously given us the grass and foliage as a relief from the warmth of the summer sun. The complement of green is red.

> *"And through the gaps of leaning trees*
> *Its mountain cradle shows,*
> *The gold against the amethyst,*
> *The green against the rose."*
> —*Whittier*

The Tertiary Colors

IF three primary colors are combined in 3 equal strengths the result is a neutral gray. But if one color predominates and the other two are about equally subservient, a grayed value of the strongest color will be produced.

When yellow is dominant, and red and blue about equal to each other, we have sage or, more lucidly speaking, gray yellow. If red is the strongest, and blue and yellow subordinate, the product is plum, or gray red. Blue in strongest value, and yellow and red each weaker, will give gray blue.

These grayed, or complex colors, with their almost endless ramifications, due to varying proportions, give us the most lasting pleasures of anything which the eye can sense. All greens in nature have red in them, all reds have some measure of green, all blues are grayed with some orange, and practically all violets have just a tinge of yellow, to make even the violet more pleasing. The more gray a color becomes, the more complex the nervous effort to sense it; the more, therefore, it appeals to the intellect, to reason and the powers of comparison. The choice beauty of the Persian rug is due to this soft graying of its component colors.

Perhaps no more happy example of tertiary coloring could lie cited than Munkácsy's "The Blind Milton Dictating PARADISE LOST to his Daughters", a large canvas which hangs in the galleries of the Lenox Library in New York. Not a single primary and not a pure secondary occur anywhere in the painting. All is in most felicitous keeping with the sublime character of the subject. One can almost feel the grand strophes and the "no mean heights" of that exalted work of poetry just by looking at the painter's work. There is also another smell canvas in the same gallery, picturing a Venetian scene, in which a single touch of orange is the nearest approach to elementary color.

Color Quality and Quantity

THREE factors enter into the determination of color quality; viz., hue, value, and chroma or intensity, as there are three factors in connection with tone (i.e., pitch, intensity, and duration), three in connection with light (i.e., wave length, wave amplitude, and wave complexity), and three in the realm of the electric current—voltage, amperage, and ohmage.

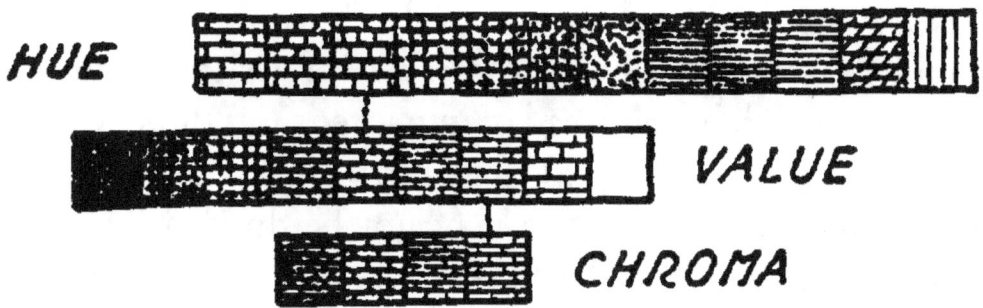

Hue has to do with the chromatic scale of primary and binary colors, ranging from pure yellow as the highest note to pure violet as the deepest. But any one hue on the chromatic scale can be diluted with either white or black, thus forming tints and shades respectively, ranging all the way from almost white to almost black. All these tones (either the normal color or its tints and shades) we call values of the given normal color. A new scale is formed by this process, very much as a singer ascertains his own "register", then sings the scale within his own range and with his own personal quality of note. Or it is perhaps more nearly comparable with a musical key. But any value of any hue can be grayed by the addition of its complement, and thus the intensity or luminosity of the original tone is reduced.

A color dictionary has been published with some thirty thousand hues, values, and intensities printed and designated.

This means that instead of the twelve hues shown here, there would be, say, sixty; instead of seven values there would be, say, fifty of each hue; instead of two intensities there would be, say, ten. This would make the thirty thousand, though the hues, values, and intensities may not be divided in just that proportion. Probably the trained eye can discern twice this many tones, but they would not be practical for present-day commercial purposes.

Mass is, of course, the sole distinction as to quantity; but it is important. A small amount of brilliant red might be very pleasing, but a great quantity abhorrent.

THOSE students of Nature who believe in God as an intelligent and personal Cause back of all the marvelous and multitudinous effects which the senses perceive, quite naturally expect to find in all of God's handiwork the stamp of his own character or personality. Even with puny man, his work bears his impress. But the work is not the man. Neither is God's work God — as Pantheism would have us believe.

Having seen the general significance of the basis or primary colors, it would be entirely in line with our expectations to discover a more than distant relationship between Color, Sound and Form.

Independent vocal sounds we call vowels — sounds which are basic and can be pronounced without the aid of another sound. American and English text books give us *a, e, i, o, u* as our vowels; but *i* is plainly a diphthong compounded of *ah* and *ee*. *Ee* is the sharpest of vowels and is avoided by vocalists, being too penetrating to he called musical, on a prominent note. There is danger that it may degenerate into a squeak. A little reflection will establish the close relationship between *ee* and a bar of glistening, penetrating, white light, perhaps hexagonal in shape.

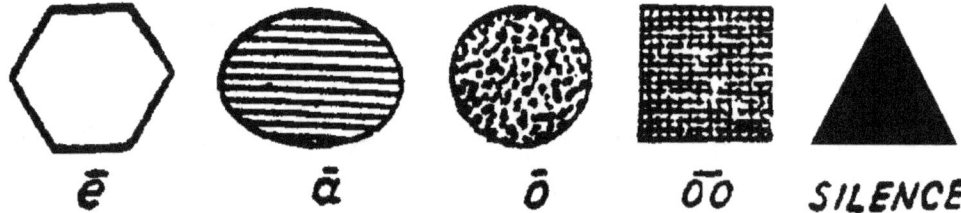

Of the basic sounds, *a*, *o*, and *oo* are left. (Note that the simpler Latin value is here given to *u*, and not the diphthong value *ee-oo*, as generally used by the English, and still to a limited extent by Americans.) *A* is a broad, elliptical, yellow sound. Of these three basic, colorful tones, it is the most brilliant, though much more mellow than *e*. *O* is a full round, red, glowing sound — the tone of love and its anguish. The bass round *oo* is blue and quadrangular, or at least angular in its configuration. Black, producing no color effect, corresponds to silence and the quiescent triangle.

All of these sounds may be understood, in concrete instances, to be not merely planes in form, but rather solids, spheroidal, spherical, cubical and pyramidal. It will be noticed that there is a fair similarity between the "shape" of these basic sounds and the shape into which the lips are brought when forming them.

Chromo-Phono-Geometric Co-ordinates

NOT only is there a similitude existing between basic colors, basic sounds and basic forms, but the parallelism extends to the more complex tones and figures. The secondary and tertiary colors are merely modifications of some primary color, formed by the addition of another primary, or a secondary, as the case may be. If a tertiary color be modified into a tint or a shade by the addition of white or black, respectively, the product is a quaternary.

All of the secondary colors, some of the tertiaries and perhaps one quaternary (light brown) are identifiable in the realm of phonetics. Between incomprehensibly rapid vibrations of white light and the absence of pulsation in dead black lies the gamut of lesser vibrations. The same remark applies to the domain of sound: between the high, piercing *e* and the point where vibration ceases to be perceived or, perhaps, ceases to exist. These delicate gradations are not so easy to trace in geometric forms. But our inability to trace them by no means disproves their existence. Nature makes use of fully as many figures as colors and sounds.

It will be noticed that of all the vowel combinations, those with the elements corresponding to red and yellow are the most frequent. Yellow is *light*; red is *action*. Apparently here in man's speech we have another index of his disposition toward ambition and struggle. Members of the *u* group of vowels are much rarer, and in Japan's cherry-blossom-chrysanthemum language are almost entirely eliminated. This suggests a dearth of the cool, reflective faculties.

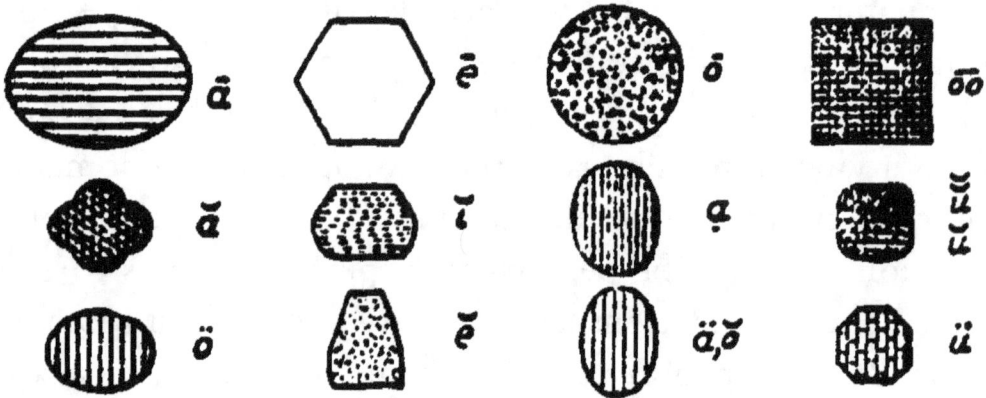

All of nature's lavish contributions to our happiness through sight, hearing and touch are drawn from these omnipresent storehouses of color, sound and form. It is not too much to say that a complete understanding of all human history, grand and lowly, would be within our grasp had we the sense to perceive and the judgment to arrange our perceptions in these fields. While all these colors, hues, shades and tints. abound in nature they somehow manage to blend in pleasing harmony, which is more than can be said of many of our attempts at creation.

> *"Flowers of all hue are struggling into glow*
> *Along the blooming fields, yet their sweet strife*
> *Melts into one harmonious concord."*
> —*Schiller*

Diphthongs and Triphthongs in Color

A diphthong, as the name suggests, is the compound sound produced by binding two vowels together by rapid successive pronunciation, still retaining a certain measure of identity with respect to the component parts. In this they differ from the vowel modifications delineated in the preceding article. To draw an illustration from the world of chemistry: a diphthong or a triphthong is a mixture of two or three sound elements, respectively; whereas the foregoing vowel modifications constitute solutions, so to speak.

In the color parallels to these vowel sounds, however, there seems to be no way of making the distinction between a modification and a diphthong—each is shown by a blending of the two elements. *E-u* (pronounced as *yu* in *yule*) is, of course, merely a tint of *u* or blue.

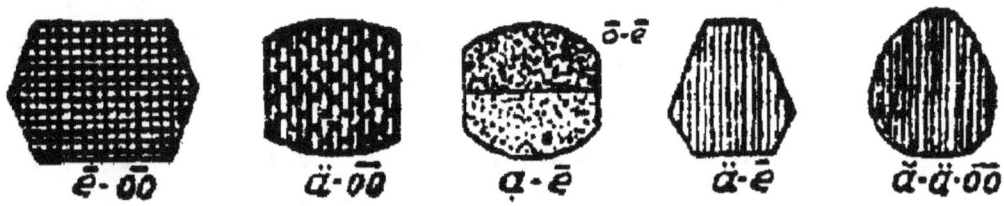

A-u (pronounced as *ow* in *owl*) is the most restful sound, as green is the tranquil color. The diphthong *a-u* indicated above has a tinge of the *o* sound, even as green, except the crudest values, always has some red to deepen it and to make the pleasing effect more lasting. Rarely, if ever, does Nature display a green unmodified by red. In certain parts of Great Britain, New England and the Southern States this diphthong is pronounced *a-u*, especially by feminine lips. *A-u* abounds in the languages of the Indo-Germanic peoples, who tend to be philosophic, but is a rarity in the Latin tongues, whose users are much more emotional—having a larger ad-mixture of vivacity (red) in their tribal character.

The twin diphthongs *o-e* and *a-e* are barely distinguishable, the *o-e* being used almost exclusively by Hebrews who have spoken more Yiddish than any other language. The *a-e* blend (pronounced as *oi* in *oil*) is most frequent in the Northern languages, even as pink is a delicately cool color.

A-e (as *I* in *isle*) is a perhaps all too frequent sound among English-speaking peoples, but it is not notably offensive, as buff is an inoffensive yet durable color. The apparently impossible triphthong *a-a-u* is the analysis of the closed English pronunciation of *o*, a sound so foreign to American ears, yet not without a rich, contemplative beauty.

Color and Tone Pitch

FROM the warm white light of the coloratura soprano's high *e* to the darksome shades of the basso profundo one can discern all the hues of color save greens; and these are formed the commingling of soprano and bass. Perhaps the most notable example of green landscape depiction in voice is the duet from Haydn's Creation, "By Thee with Bliss." The warm, mellow sunshine of the treble part blends into the cooling shadows of the bass. The restful undulations of the landscape are flecked here with bright patches of new verdure, there with the quiet shadows of a tranquil pool. Eve's pleasing perception joins with Adam's righteous judgment in a hymn of praise and adoration to their Maker.

Soprano merges into the yellow orange of mezzo-soprano, and mezzo-soprano into the orange of alto. The mellowness of alto is due to

its two constituent parts — light and action, wisdom and love. A soprano and tenor duet, such as Puccini's "The Power of Love" (in La Boheme), produces the general color effect of orange but has more interest than a single orange voice because of the harmony of the two parts, each of which maintains its own quality.

Tenor is unquestionably the voice of love, of love that moves things. In mediæval times the tenor always carried the air, and such is still frequently the case — wellnigh always in ballads, the songs of love and adventure. It is well fitted for such a role because of its position in the center of the chromatic scale, as love is the actuating principle in the midst of human experience.

The violet tones of the baritone voice are best suited for subjects of majestic sweep, love tinged with the shadows of life, love refined with sorrow. Bass runs into the still deeper shadows as exemplified by such semi-popular songs as "Asleep in the Deep," "Rocked in the Cradle of the Deep," and "The Sexton's Song."

In color, as in tone, pulsation and cadence enter into symphony. The various keys furnish modifications inside a given register and allow ample scope for the expression of both basic and transient moods of individual character.

Color and the Compass

MOST of the world's history has been made in the Northern Hemisphere, and it is for this reason that the symbolic import of directions has always given to the North the characteristic of cold and to the South that of warmth. Many peoples and tribes of the earth have personified the directions of the compass: but none, perhaps, more picturesquely than have the Algonquin Indians, who refer to the various cardinal winds as "the fierce Kabibanoka" (North); "the gentle Wauban" (East); "Shawandassee, fat and lazy" (South); and "the mighty Mudjekeewis" (West).

In Scriptural symbolism North represents the seat of divine empire — "promotion cometh not from the east, nor from the west, nor from the south" — and the foundation or establishment of God's throne is *Justice* (Psalm 89:14, margin) East represents the redemptive work of Christ, the motive or actuating principle of

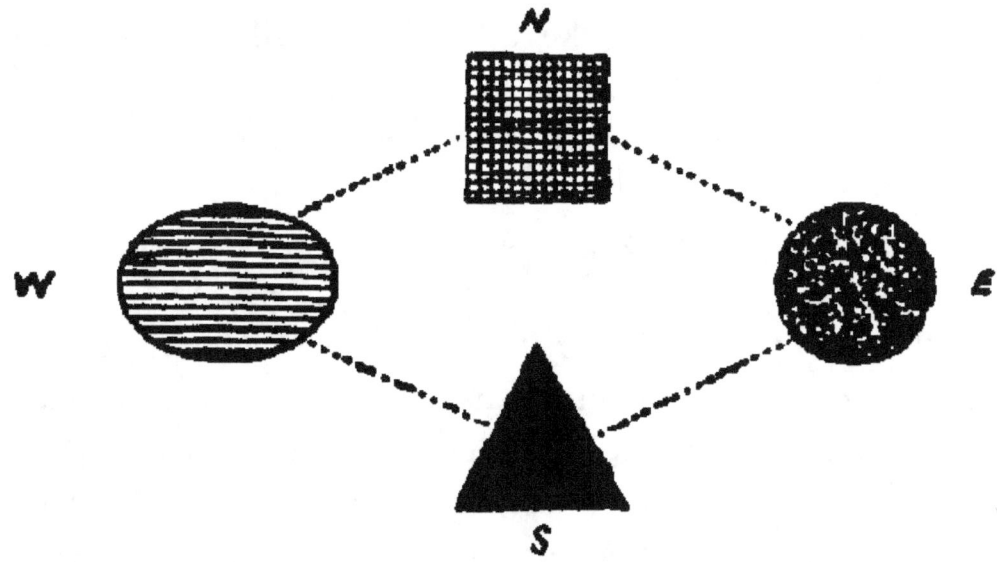

which is *Love.* (John 3:16) South seems to have reference to humanity. To the Christian it has a double meaning: black is in some respects a picture of death, and to the followers of Christ human hopes are dead: black is a symbol of power, the power that is necessary for the bringing of blessings to humanity and the sole characteristic of God which has not been manifested in large measure to the world. On this fulcrum of *Power* are all the other cardinal principles balanced and sustained. Christ "upholds all things by the word of his power" and "through *death* he shall destroy him that hath the power of death, that is the devil."—Hebrews 1:4; 2:14.

The West is the golden gate to wisdom, sought in vain by the world by its own means and methods ("The world by [its] wisdom knew not God"), but attained in truth by Christ, the High Priest, and His faithful underpriests as they journey through the antitypical Tabernacle to the brilliant Shekinah glory of God's all-embracing perception where "we shall know even as also we are known."—1 Corinthians 13:12.

There is also a certain analogy existing between the directions and the seasons. North can hardly be other than Winter; East, Spring; South, Summer: and West, Fall. Spring is the buoyant, fecund season; Summer the fruitful season; Fall the accounting season; and Winter the quiescent time. Black seems an anomaly in thinking of Summer. It is not, however, a picture of the atmosphere, but a *symbol* of the potentiality or dynamic force working in the fruit-bearing qualities of all nature.

Color and the Elements

THE ancients recognized four basic elements in the cosmogony of things—air, earth, fire, and water. They also connected these with basic elements of character, though it does not appear whether they carried the analogy further.

Air corresponds, without any violence done to the fitness of things, to yellow in color, light in life, wisdom in character, buoyancy in conduct, cheerfulness in disposition, and hope among the graces. It is the yellowness in the atmosphere that draws the crocuses from the ground in Spring; it is the same yellow air in Summer that ripens the grains and fruits, for the bluish gray days have no ripening power. The yellow, bright days are the cheerful ones, everytime.

   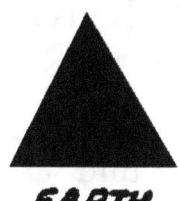

AIR   WATER   FIRE   EARTH

Water finds analogy in blue as to color, shadow in life, justice in character, stability or dignity in conduct, reticence in disposition, and faith among the graces. As justice is the great stabilizer, so is water the great stabilizing medium among human needs. It modifies a fever, tends to equalize the temperature of the globe, and its continued presence in the form of rain or dew has actually contributed to all the periods of brilliant human achievement and development which the world has known. It is used as a Scriptural figure of justice and blessing for the people.

Fire correlates with red in color, action in life, love in character, vivacity in conduct, affability in disposition, and charity among the graces. Fire is the moving element in the physical world as love is the motive principle in human experience — love, even though perverted into self-love, or else love for an improper object.

Earth parallels black in color, inertness in life, force in character, static in conduct, and taciturnity in disposition. The earth is the means by which, perhaps it were more accurate to say the agency without which the other elements could not operate in connection with human affairs. So power is not, strictly speaking, a characteristic, but is rather a capacity for performance in connection with the other elements of character.

Color and Temperament

FOR modern, practical purposes classification of people into three groups, vital, motive, and mental, is sufficiently accurate. However, some finer analyses are possible; though the other divisions, with the exception of phlegmatic, are really secondary or binary in their natures, because partaking of two other basic temperaments. Other names have appeared in both ancient and near-modern psychological literature, but they are identifiable as one or another of those pictured above. Motive was formerly, though unhappily, called bilious—or more properly fibrous — and its perversion was sometimes referred to as choleric; the mental was better known as melancholic; and the nervous occasionally denominated classical.

In attempting to classify the organisms of mankind it is essential at the outset to recognize the fact that there are no absolute types. Every one has some vital, some motive and some mental qualities in his makeup; but one of these may predominate so noticeably as to serve for a type. If two qualities are about balanced, and the third of small force, life in that individual will take on a violet, an orange, or a greenish cast, acording to the component elements.

The vital temperament is characterized by rotundity of organism and an indisposition to marked activity. Persons of this type make much better managers than workers. Strength in and activity of the abdominal viscera pre-dominate over that of other body parts.

The motive temperament, as the name implies, abounds in action. Whereas with people of the vital stamp movement is a luxury, with those of the motive strain movement is both a necessity and a comfort. In this temperament the muscular portion of the system predominates in activity and is evinced by strongly marked and firmly set features, firmness of flesh, moderate fulness: the general functional activity extends also to the brain.

The mental temperament is that in which the purely intellectual activities preponderate. People of this class tend to the shadow side of life; they are not able to radiate cheerfulness, because they do not possess it. They manifest, on the psychical side, deep and enduring sensibility; the fancy, as arising from receptivity, predominates in these passive people. The feeling is disposed to sadness; desire shows itself more as yearning. Men eminent in art and science fall usually into this class.

"When I compare the season of youth (not childhood) to the melancholy temperament, you will perhaps be astonished and ask whether youth is not the time of pleasure. But it is, above all other ages, the age of the ideal; and this is the feature which places the young among the melancholy. They mentally build up a world of their own — an ideal world, of which their fervid imagination is enamored — and deem themselves to be raised far above the common-place world around. There is something lovable in this youthful disposition; and we ought all to keep young in this sense, in which it has been well said that they who grow old never were young. But the danger in this stage is the pride which despises others, and that revelling in fancy and sentiment which, shunning real earnest work, seeks its ideal in enjoyment, and at last in very un-ideal enjoyment. Manhood is the time of work. . . . Our will contends against the resistance offered by actual life, and strives to master it." —Luthardt.

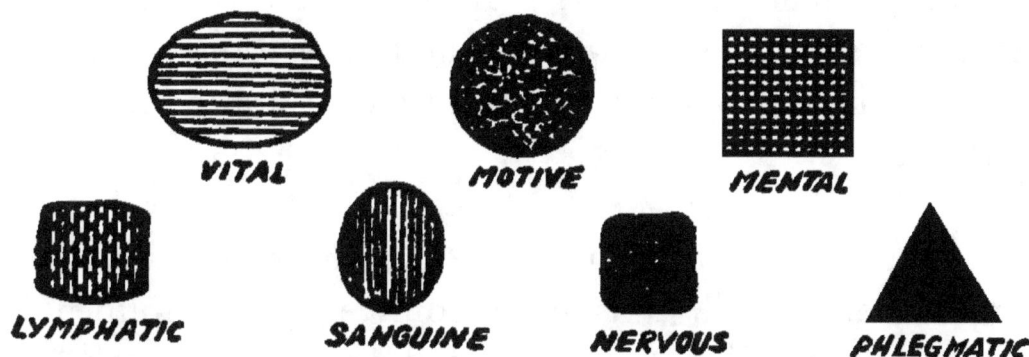

VITAL MOTIVE MENTAL

LYMPHATIC SANGUINE NERVOUS PHLEGMATIC

The phlegmatic temperament is the direct antithesis of the motive. In it action, so far from being a necessity or comfort of life, is a positive extravagance. Perhaps no more perfect example of this type could be found than the old darkey who was observed day after day to sit at his cabin door in a state of lassitude so complete that he did not even draw on his drooping pipe, in which the fires of industry had long since died out: on being asked by a passerby what he did, the old man, after much deliberation, made answer: "Well, sah — sometimes ah sets and thinks — and sometimes, ah jest sets." But even this is not a perfect type: for he confessed to a slight tinge of the mental. The truly phlegmatic, like the pyramid, "jest set."

The nervous or sensitive temperament confers great quickness and vivacity of mental action, without a corresponding capability of endurance. The brain is so active that it is very easily excited and, for the want of endurance, soon exhausts its powers. The most exquisite examples of it are found in the female sex.

The sanguine is, in many respects, the most interesting temperament of all. It is most completely exemplified in childhood and is indicated by well-defined forms, moderate plumpness of person, tolerable firmness of flesh and ruddiness of countenance. The vital processes are carried on rapidly; consumption and reproduction quickly alternate, the circulation is brisk, predominating in the arteries, the nerves are irritable, the movements light, and fancy is more or less prevalent in the operations of the mind. While this temperament disposes to openness and frankness and in susceptibility to the most various impressions, it opposes at the same time great hindrances to the fulfillment of duty; for it disposes to flightiness, to superficiality, and so to split up life into an unconnected multiplicity. Orange is the richest color in the world, but it lacks staying power.

The lymphatic is the restful temperament, as green is the restful color. It inclines to be the procrastinating temperament. It may be a devoté of the *mañana* gospel, whose litany, put into

Cumberland mountainese, reads: "There's a whole day tomorry that ain't teched yit." Such an individual is not easily roused to exertion, and even if roused, soon sinks into a lull again. He may be capable of great things but seldom attains therm. He prefers to browse around in fields more philosophic than practical.

Color and Its Maker

PERFECT character is perfect balance, or nicety of poise between the qualities of a perfect being. Jehovah's character is not only the perfect standard but also the fountainhead of all character qualities. Some animals lower than man have certain items of character plainly marked; and these qualities are made use of in inspired and uninspired literature as illustrations of desirable traits, often too lacking in fallen man.

Wisdom, justice, love and power have long been recognized by careful students of the Bible as being the cardinal principles or characteristics of God, the Ruler of the universe. Some students have magnified His justice in such a way as to imply a dearth of wisdom and love. Others have talked of His love, as though justice were not coexistent. And still others, by intimating failure of His "efforts," slander His wisdom and power. None can fully sense His power, though some minds can believe that it exists and that it is continually manifest in the works of Nature, both animate and inanimate.

Wisdom, justice and love are readily recognizable as being abstract principles, but power seems just a little different. It is more like the thumb to a three-fingered hand, or the base pole of an electric controller. Without it not one of the character elements can function. The honest difficulty in seeing black as a symbol of divine power is the statement of St. John: "He is light; and in him is no darkness at all." Nevertheless, He made "thick darkness" to be swaddling clothes for the earth. The only solution seems to be that His personal, subjective self knows no darkness, as light contains no black, but that the character picture which He has chosen to give us is exemplified through His works rather than immediately. Though in light there is neither black nor white, yet in pigments there is black: and in Nature black is certainly indicative of strength – especially of character strength.

Each of these elements has an abstract and a concrete, a theoretic and a practical phase. The inert phase of wisdom is knowledge: but when wisdom is called upon to consider a single problem it cannot do so without the coöperation of power. *Discretion* is applied wisdom, and the very application calls for effort, is not possible without it. *Truth* is the precept of justice; but its practice becomes *righteousness* — for the practice power must lend a helping hand. *Benevolence* is passive love, the very minimum of that noble trait; but an active love we call *beneficence*. Even power itself may be latent, *might*, or kinetic, *force*.

It is also interesting to note not only that power is necessary for the exercise of the character elements, but also that no one of these principles can be brought into action without measurable contributions from the remaining two, as well. Wisdom would not be wisdom that were deaf to justice and love; love cannot exist in all its fulness in the presence of injustice and folly; justice cannot ignore either wisdom or love, for a man is not just at all until he loves his neighbor as himself. In this connection it is appropriate to observe that rarely, if ever, does Nature display a primary color — rarely indeed a true binary. It is practically always found that some percentage of the other two primaries is discernible, even where one primary is in decided predominance.

In Jehovah all the cardinal principles work in perfect balance and accord. If man were perfect, as at the beginning, his character, too, would be in perfect balance, a true image of the perfect pattern. Even as it is there is enough fragmentary testimony in unbalanced man to enable him to appreciate these qualities and their beauty. In the perfect life love prompts, wisdom devises, justice directs, and power performs every act.

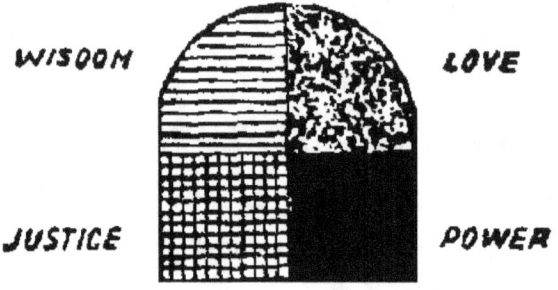

As yellow is the illuminating color, so wisdom is the illuminating quality in a character. Hope is the outgrowth of wisdom, and joy is the outgrowth of hope — and yellow is the cheerful, happy color. Wisdom therefore, may be called the yellow, the pleasant sunshine, of character. Blue is the cool, the shadow color: and justice is the reserved, the restrictive, the directive phase of character. Nothing else than justice could "mark the bounds of habitation" and say to the sea: "Thus far shalt thou come, and no further." Would it be incongruous to speak of justice as the blue, the true blue of character? Faith is inseparable from justice; for faith is belief in integrity. As red is the color of action so love is the moving or motive principle among the others. Love is the thing hoped for, of which faith is the foundation. All the warmth there is in the world comes from love, all the cheer and light from wisdom, and all the dependability and uprightness from justice.

Color and the Messiah

"IN Him [Christ] all fulness dwells." Since Jesus, the Christed or Anointed, is "the express image of his [God's] person" it is but natural to expect that the same principles which work so harmoniously in the Father should also be found in the Son. But the word Messiah, or Christ, has a broader application than merely to the individual Jesus. It is used in the New Testament as applying to the Christ class, the glorified church, sharing with Jesus, under His headship, the glories and privileges of rule in Messiah's kingdom.

This Messiah class, during the thousand years of its reign, will fill a three-fold office of prophet, priest and king — successfully counteracting the baneful influences of the present triple alliance of the world, the flesh and the devil. As the prophet the Messiah will teach the people, as priest He will intercede for them, and as king He will rule them with unparalleled justice and power.

It is manifest that for the proper conducting of so grand an office as prophet for all mankind wisdom is a prime prerequisite. Furthermore, it requires superhuman wisdom to be able to discern with unerring perception what to teach, when to teach and how to teach it. To fulfil properly the office of priest will require oceans of love: for almost unbounded patience and benevolence will he necessary to deal with all the shortcomings of man, both willful and unintended. A perfect king must be able to exercise both justice and power. And the great Messiah king shall not fail: for "when thy judgments are in the earth, the inhabitants of the world will learn righteousness."

It is singularly worthy of observation that the divine wisdom of the divinely appointed prophet is just what is needed to abrogate the claims which the present social system of the world makes on a human being. "The world by [its] wisdom has not known God," therefore, "the wisdom of their wise men shall perish, and the understanding of their prudent men shall fail." Nothing but the fathomless billows of divine love can master the present partly depraved desires and penchants of the individual flesh; and only the power and justice of the King of kings can deal adequately with Satan, the prince of the adversaries of God.

The Messiah class, Christ the head and the church, His body, is shown under another beautiful figure as consisting of the second Adam and a second Eve. The kingly and basic qualities of Jehovah's character are justice and power ("righteousness is the establishment of his throne") and the queenly crowning qualities are wisdom and love. Justice and power cooperating produce authority — neither can do it alone. Wisdom and love working together harmoniously produce splendor, even as orange is the most splendid color.

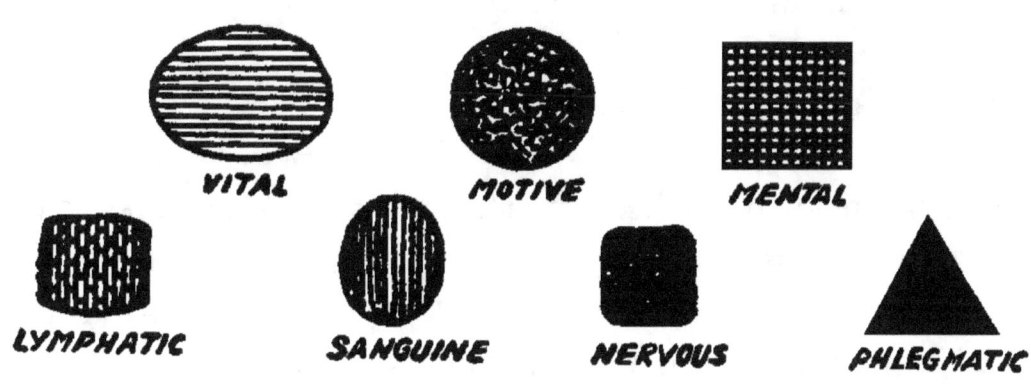

VITAL   MOTIVE   MENTAL

LYMPHATIC   SANGUINE   NERVOUS   PHLEGMATIC

If the crowning, queenly qualities seem to outshine the more sombre-hued kingly traits, and thus appear to bring more glory to the church than to her Lord, it must be remembered that she is His glory. "She is a crown of glory and a royal diadem in the hand of our God." Furthermore if, even in her perfect state, she had the longing to bless and the wisdom to bless mankind she could not do it without His power, for "without him she can do nothing" — "He is the head over all things to the church, which is his body". Nor can it be forgotten that that very desire to bless and that very knowledge of how to bless came from Him; for He "of God is made unto us wisdom, righteousness, sanctification [the fruitage of love], and redemption," the trophy of power. Therefore, the church does not outshine nor even equal the beauty of Him who is "fairer than the sons of men." He, in turn, is glorious because He is Jehovah's image.

Heart, Mind, Soul, Strength

JESUS, the great teacher, ratified the current epitome of the Godward side of the law to Israel which said: "Thou shalt love the Lord thy God with all thy heart, and with all thy mind, and with all thy soul, and with all thy strength." Evidently He meant to convey the thought that love for and worship of Jehovah should not be one-sided, but all-sided —

that it should engross to the fullest capacity every power of mind and body.

The "heart" evidently includes the sentiments and emotions — love as it finds utterance in the human life. Sentiment is feeling, a perception of personal weal or woe; while emotion is the effect produced on the nervous system by strong sentiment. Sentiment is the river flow, now placid and deep, now shallow and noisy; emotion is the dammed-back water head, used here, perhaps, to drive something useful, there merely to flow over the dam or to tear it from its moorings.

 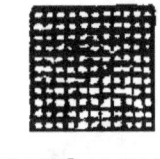  

SENTIMENT   JUDGMENT   PERCEPTION   ORGANISM

The "mind" would seem to have reference to the reflective powers, the judgment, the capacity for decision on right and wrong, to measurable ability to introduce equity by such decision. The judgment is good or bad, helpful or harmful, in proportion as it is aligned with justice, the divine and perfect standard, without acquaintanceship with which no mind can glorify God or enjoy Him forever.

The "soul" is another way of referring to the sentient powers or the perceptions, the moral perceptions in particular. Perception in general is the conscious reference of a sensation to the cause which produced it; it is wisdom, discernment of right and wrong in their relationship to happiness and unhappiness.

Strength depends not so much on either muscular energy or nervous force alone as on a proper balance between the two. But at all events "strength" refers to the organism, the means or agency at our disposal for carrying out what the heart prompts, the soul perceives, or the mind directs. In fact, neither sentiment, judgment, nor perception can function without the cooperation of organism.

The greater the *balance* existing between these four powers the greater the individual's capacity to love God, because he will have more in common with God. The priceless power to restore lost balances, or to reinstate a temporarily disturbed balance, we call *humor* — or ability to see one's self in proper perspective and to realize one's actual, not imagined, relationship to other persons and things. No imperfect creature can attain a perfect balance without divine aid; and even then not while he remains imperfect.

Color and the Fine Arts

THE basic qualities of character which were in perfect power and accord in father Adam, and which now are fragmentary and more or less discordant, find their expression in the best efforts man has made to comprehend the æsthetic things of earth. For art is expression of character.

In suggesting a certain analogy between the fine arts, the basic colors and the character qualities which enable one to appreciate or to work in fine arts it must be carefully borne in mind that it is a generalized grouping, indicating rather the tendency of the various arts to grow out of and appeal to a given trait of character.

Poetry, or perhaps it would be better to say literature, is the most rarified form of art. But even in those ethereal fields there are decided differences of atmospheric pressure, according to the subject matter treated. It may deal with things so low as to come well within the zone of smoke and grime; it may circle in and out among the tree-tops, touch the chilly summit, or sweep the ocean clean.

Music, "the voice of love," may vary as much as love itself. Italy is the land of vehement, emotional music; France, that of sentimental and yet intellectual symphony; Germany, the country of profound philosophical meditations in harmony.

Painting and sculpture, manifestly the more material arts, seem to identify themselves particularly with intellect and organism. In both arts there are the idealistic and the realistic schools, in which intellect and emotion predominate respectively. There is the ultra-idealism of Rodin and the realism of ancient sculptors. There is the ultra-idealism of Turner and the realism of the Middle Ages. Somewhere in between lies the most satisfying ground.

POETRY   MUSIC   PAINTING   SCULPTURE

In literature and music attempt is made to express the concrete world abstractly; while with painting and sculpture (in which is included architecture) attempt is made to express the abstract world concretely. Each art opens up a new world and becomes a new language.

To respond to emotional excitation requires less effort than to exercise the intellect; so it is only natural that the majority of people should show most interest in those forms of art in which feeling is the most prominent quality, The popular French artist Millet supplies an example of this sort of art in the field of painting; Mendelssohn in music; Dickens in literature. No one can question the genius of these men, yet they do not carry one so far into the lofty heights of intellect as do, for instance, Whistler, Schoenberg, and Poe.

But the extreme of too much thought and too little feeling in the field of the fine arts is fully as undesirable as the same unbalanced state in character. Where thought and feeling are perfectly balanced the most happy results are secured. And the four men whose works are looked upon as meeting this test are Balzac, the litterateur; Bach, the symphonist; Rembrandt, the painter; and Michaelangelo, the sculptor. Perhaps no one, outside of divine supervision, surpasses the creations of these four giants.

The cardinal excellence, then, in great art, as in great character, is perfect balance. And, indeed, without considerable balance of character, no real æsthetic understanding of art is possible. For in order to understand art it is necessary to recreate the work of art in one's mind, rebuilding the æsthetic structure by the same successive steps followed by its creator, as he, in turn, followed the original Creator.

Color and Physiognomy

INDIVIDUALITY is polarized in the face. Emotional, mental, moral, and physical states of being are unfailingly mirrored there. Not only are the passing emotions pictured on this sensitive screen, but the four basic principles of all intelligent and morally responsible life have permanent citadels on the visage of man — in perfect man a veritable uninvadable tetrarchy.

The eyes, "the windows of the soul," are the most delicately responsive centers of perception — inquiring, inviting, retiring, inciting. If there is "nobody home" inside there will be no lights at the windows. No one has lived very long who does not know the power of a single glance to ravish the senses of a whole roomful of people. Yellow is the color of wisdom, and yellow in the normal coloring of the eye has from time immemorial been recognized as indicative of sagacity, astuteness, acumen. As a matter of course, there are no wholly yellow eyes, but it will be borne in mind that yellow is one of the principal constitutents of brown and hazel. Furthermore, it is often observed in a gray eye that yellowish rays emanate as from the pupil toward the circumference of the iris.

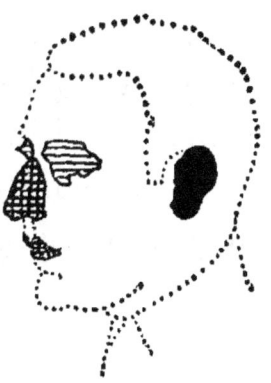

A "blue nose" is a symbol of austerity, with perhaps a prudish tinge. Both of these qualities are but perversions of justice — lines of conduct wherein conscience predominates over common sense. The size of the nose, as also the size of the eyes, is not without significance. The small-nosed man cannot have a judicial mind, whatever his other excellencies may be. And a man whose nose upturns can no more be expected to administer justice than a pug dog can be expected to act as a shepherd.

"Ruby lips" need no introduction as the stronghold of love, the fortress of sensuous perception. Their covering merges from the epidermal tissue of the outer body to the epithelial lining of the inner organism; and on this rosy frontier more of the world's history than is suspected has been fraught. The thick lip is the sensual lip ; the large mouth is the generous mouth. The small mouth knows no love.

Now comes the black ear! What maternal solicitude has been directed to its eradication, and here it is justifying its existence as the base of power. It occupies a position about equally distant from the three other poles. But what-ever its color, its size and position and setting are certainly indicative of force. The orifice of the ear in the fully balanced man is said to be in the geometric center of the profile head.

Color and Sex

GOD is the author and source of every principle in creation; and every principle in creation must inhere in Him, either actively or passively. "He that made the eye; shall he not see: he that made the ear; shall he not hear?" Likewise He that made man in His own image and afterward separated him into two sexes, or sections, must Himself have all the qualities which He gave them, either jointly or severally. His fatherly love exceeds that of the fondest parent, and His motherly care is in no wise equalled by the tenderest nurturer of babes.

MAN   WOMAN

Adam and Eve, before their transgression, were each perfect parts of a complete microcosm, whose aggregate qualities were in the same relation to each other as those in God. The separation left the masculine virtues of justice and power largely predominant in man, while the feminine graces of wisdom and love were much more pronounced in woman.

Masculinity is marked by straight lines; femininity abounds in curves. A straight line is the shortest distance between two points, and the direct line is the masculine way of going about things. It is no attempt at facetiousness to say that a curved line is one that changes its direction at every point. The feminine way of doing things is by tact, a deft fitting of self to the circumstances, a bending of self around the sharp masculine corners. True, there are tactful men and hopelessly direct women; but it will be found that one or the other feminine trait is ascendant in such men, or that justice and power lead in such women.

As wisdom and love are the feminine qualities, so yellow and red are feminine colors. Golden hair and rosy cheeks are certainly emblematic of maidenhood; black hair and blue eyes symbolic of virile youth, as black and blue are analogous to power and justice.

The diagrammatic depiction of the sexes shown above is of course abstract and theoretic. It represents the balance which would exist between a perfect couple. Needless to observe, the character outlines of most pairs would be notably divergent from this. If masculinity predominated in both man and woman, they might understand one another well (perhaps too well) ; but there would be small *complementary* association.

If perchance wisdom and justice prevail in one person and love and power in the other, the character of the first will be marked by reason and that of the second by emotion – not a bad combination for business purposes, but rather unsatisfactory in marriage.

The Cains and Abels

THE general division of mankind into male and female is universally recognized. But that division is one depending more on organism than on character; it depends on character only insofar as character is influenced by organism and conventional social demands. Another grand division is subtler and yet hardly less important in the attempt to understand Man.

The division, for want of a better name, may be called the Cain and Abel grouping because these men are prominent prototypes of the classes existing. The same division, in a way, is noticeable between Adam and Eve at their first transgression of divine law. But because of a desire to preserve them as pictures of the perfect division which God made, and because of the fact that they were of different sexes, it would be perhaps less complex to take their two sons as examples.

In Cain wisdom and power, sagacity and brute force, were the outstanding features of character. Love and justice were very, very small in his poor character. He was a red-blooded fighting man, if you please — a go-getter, a Terrible Ted. No supine waiting on the Lord for him; no searching of divine counsel. All he asked of God was to be let alone; he was quite capable of doing the rest. Neither did he wish to be disturbed by any baby prattlings about moral responsibility. Clear the decks for *action!* was his motto. He became a captain of industry and is the idol of the ambitious and the somebodies in that realm, as he is the idol of every warrior in earth's first act of violence.

On the other hand was Abel, the slain. In his character justice and love stand out. He loved God enough to be faithful to Him; and he loved his brother enough to suggest how he, too, might have divine favor. Abel was a nobody (from the standpoint of the world), a nincompoop, a pacifist as regarded his personal safety. Perhaps there have been more Abels than Cains, but the world knows little about them. And the world knows little about them because it does not care to know about them. Its Abels have hidden in dens and caves of the earth, been stoned, sawn asunder, and slain with the sword. Their blood has been shed on crosses, it has sotted the sands of the Roman

Coliseum and Circus; and in smaller and much less conspicuous ways they have suffered martyrdom at the hand of the Cains.

Is it any wonder that but few of the true followers of Christ have been chosen from the great ones of earth? Wisdom and power are about all that is left of the once splendid character of Satan; love and justice he has perverted, but prefers to discard them altogether.

Wisdom and love people, whether male or female, are more interested in *who's* right than in *what's* right, more taken with personalities than with principles. Wisdom and power people make things hum; if women, they display a decided penchant toward wearing the — toga of authority.

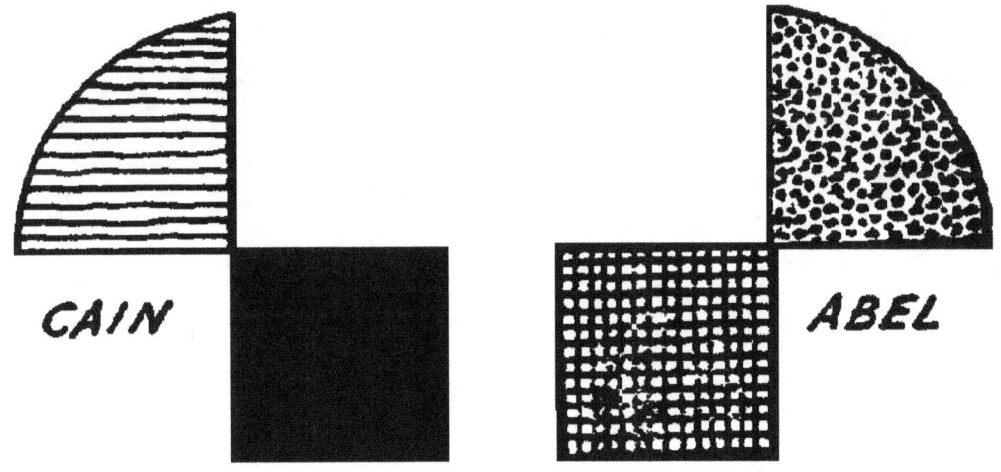

Love furnishes all the tenderness there is in life; justice all the honesty and straightforwardness.

But the tragic mistake of any one, and especially of the Christian, is to think that his character state, whatever it may be, is necessarily a fixed thing. It is not so. No matter what it was, it can be made more nearly balanced, and hence more glorious in the Father's sight, "according to that working whereby he is able to subdue all things, even unto himself."

Color and World Empire

MORE than 2,500 years ago God, through the Prophet Daniel, gave a picture of world empire, which had begun with Nebuchadnezzar at the overthrow of Zedekiah, the last of the divinely recognized Jewish sovereigns, and which was to end with the "times of the gentiles" – A.D. 1914.

Indeed the vision was given to King Nebuchadnezzar; but inasmuch as neither he nor his wise men could interpret it, the real unfolding of its meaning was left to Daniel. And under divine guidance he told how the golden head of the great image which the king had seen was a picture of the Babylonian Empire; the silver breast and arms pictured the Miedo-Persian government; the brass belly and thighs the Empire of Grecia; and the legs of iron represented Imperial Rome.

It is notable that the value of these metals decreases from head to foot, and their hardness increases in about the same ratio. Furthermore, if exposed to the weather the gold would remain practically unchanged, the silver would tarnish, the brass would both tarnish and oxidize, while with iron the wasting by oxidation would be very considerable.

While God turned over these 2,520 years to gentile dominion it must not be thought that the gentile sovereigns have ruled according to divine laws or principles, nor that God has assumed any responsibility for their conduct. Rather it has been permitted with a view to demonstrating for all time that man, while imperfect, is incapable of governing himself, that the quality of his success has grown worse and worse, and that he is in need of the Messianic kingdom, now at the door.

Gold is not yellow, but orange yellow; and orange is the color of splendor. Babylon, though not so long-lived as the other empires, was by far the most splendid. On this point Dr. Lord says: "Babylon during its brief dominion, after having been subject to Assyria for seven hundred years, reappeared in unparalleled splendor, and was probably the most magnificent capital the ancient world ever saw until Rome arose". And there seems to be no good reason for excluding Rome from this comparison.

Media came next with Cyrus at her head. Silver is bluish; though gray, neutral as to color, is still stronger. Blue is the color of stability; so an effort was made by the Medea and Persians to have their laws immutable and applicable alike to high and low. Lord says again : "For the first time in Asia there

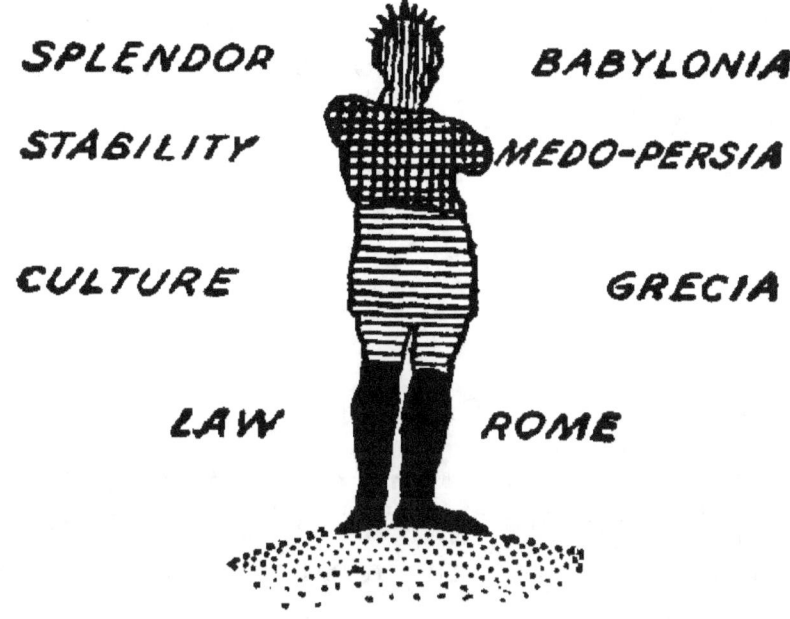

SPLENDOR   BABYLONIA

STABILITY   MEDO-PERSIA

CULTURE   GRECIA

LAW   ROME

was, on the accession of Cyrus to unlimited power, a recognition of justice, and the adoration of one supreme deity ruling in goodness and truth".

Brass is yellow, and yellow is the color of wisdom, culture. Greece sought to rule by science, philosophy, art. As the belly and thigh region contain the center of the reproductive powers, so Grecia disseminated or planted seeds of much indeed of the world's store of knowledge, and has given us the language which has perpetuated not only much error but also much truth, by far the most outstanding of which are the New Testament writings.

Pure iron is black, and black is the symbol of power. Rome's predominant characteristic was power; power exerted through her wonderful army, howbeit directed by law. With those iron legs Rome stalked through the known world and established her law.

Faith, Hope, Love

THE inspired Apostle Paul tells us that Faith, Hope and Love are abiding, basic qualities. Faith in a given promise will cease to fix itself on that promise when it is fulfilled; but faith as a quality, a belief in the integrity of God and of all His perfect creatures, will no more pass away than will the justice on which faith is built. Faith always remains true blue. Objectively, it is the foundation of things hoped for; subjectively, it is the conviction of things not seen.

Likewise hope, or avid expectation for the fulfillment of a given promise, will cease to function when that thing is attained: "for what a man hath, why doth he yet hope for it?" But the hopeful quality of the perfect character will embrace some other unaccomplished phase of God's design, always buoyant, always expectant. Hope in the Christian is traceable to the presence of heavenly wisdom. Without this holy discernment and discretion, without this ability to compare the sufferings of this present time with the glory that shall be revealed in us, the poor follower of Christ is forever plashing around in the slough of despond.

Love is the motive principle of divine character, the distinguishing principle in Jehovah's dealings with the church. Because love as a motive for action is so rare in human affairs, it is set before the mind as being the thing to strive for — "the greatest of these." It is the greatest because it is the starter. Faith itself works by love, a love of the dependable qualities we recognize in God. Furthermore, love is a possibility now; even with imperfect brains it is possible to *wish* others well, and to admire such excellencies as they may have.

FAITH HOPE LOVE

Power is not mentioned in this grouping given by the Apostle, probably for the reason that now is not the time for power. We cannot be trusted with power until we have justice, wisdom and love in perfection. The world's long experience in striving for and usurping power is one sad commentary on man's inability to exercise power without the proper balance wheels. Now we (whether high or low) are not fit to be trusted with power.

Diagrammatic Summary

Color and Form	⬭ Yellow	⬮ Orange	◉ Red	▦ Violet	◼ Blue	▤ Green	▲ Black
Objective Significance of Color	Light	Splendor	Warmth	Majesty	Shadow	Repose	Strength
Subjective Effect of Color	Cheer	Vivacity	Action	Serenity	Dignity	Rest	Power
Sound and Color	ă°	ä	ā	ŭ	ū •	ău	Silence
Tone and Color	Soprano	Alto	Tenor	Barytone	Bass	Sop. & Bass	....
Orchestral Colors	Flute	Clarinet	Coronet	Bassoon	Bass	Oboe	......
" "	Violin	Second V.	Trombone	Cello	Viol	Harp	....
Points of Compass	West	....	East	....	North	....	South
Temperaments	Vital	Sanguine	Motive	Nervous	Mental	Lymphatic	Phlegmatic
The Elements	Air	....	Fire	....	Water	....	Earth
Divine Attributes	Wisdom	....	Love	....	Justice	....	Power
Messianic Offices	Prophet	....	Priest	....	King	....	King
Worship Capacity	Soul	....	Heart	....	Mind	....	Strength
The Fine Arts	Poetry	....	Music	....	Painting	....	Sculpture
Physiognomy	Eyes	....	Lips	....	Nose	....	Ears
Sex and Color	Feminine	....	Feminine	....	Masculine	....	Masculine
World Empire	Grecia	Babylonia	....	....	Medo-Persia	....	Rome
Attempted Rule Through	Culture	Splendor	....	....	Stability	....	Law
Fruits of Spirit	Hope	....	Love	....	Faith	....	....
The Seasons	Fall	....	Spring	....	Winter	....	Summer

Glossary of Terms

AS a supplement to the foregoing observations on Color and Character we append this classified list of recognized characteristics, arranged under the headings of Wisdom, Justice, Love, and Power. Some of the attributes partake quite plainly of more than one cardinal attribute; but effort has been made to list all qualities under the principle to which they most closely belong.

This list is intended as a mere glossary of terms for convenience. All of the definitions given are obtainable in any dictionary of size.

WISDOM

That principle which both devises and counsels the selection of right ends as well as right means. WISDOM is the right use or exercise of knowledge, and differs from knowledge as sight from seeing.

1. ITS MACHINERY OR MENTAL EQUIPMENT:

(A) *Judgment*	Reason or Comparison. The comparing of ideas to find their mutual relations.
(B) *Discernment*	Accuracy and keenness of mental vision.
(C) *Discrimination*	The tracing out of minute distinctions and the nicest shades of thought.
(D) *Acuteness*	The faculty of *nice* discrimination.
(E) *Acumen*	The faculty of *quick* discernment, owing to the increase of mental stores.
(F) *Penetration*	The power of seeing *deeply* into a subject in spite of everything that intercepts the view.

2. ITS OBJECTIVE EXERCISE:

A. *DEFENSIVE: as shown in guarding, against hurtful influences and opposing forces.*

(a) *Prudence*	Using right means rather in avoiding danger than in taking decisive measures for the accomplishment of an object.
(b) *Discretion*	Judgment and *calm* thought in the proper use of the right means.
(c) *Watchfulness*	Careful and diligent observation for the purpose of preventing or escaping danger, or of avoiding mistakes and misconduct.
(d) *Vigilance*	Careful not only to escape danger but to detect evil.
(e) *Forethought*	Provision against foreseen dangers and wants.
(f) *Carefulness*	Persistently guarding against danger.
(g) *Circumspection*	Looking carefully at things all around before acting.
(h) *Cautiousness*	Prudence in regard to contingencies.

B. *OFFENSIVE: as shown in securing the material resources and comforts of life.*

(a) *Frugality*	Cuts off all unnecessaries.
(b) *Economy*	The right use of necessaries.
(c) *Thrift*	Economy and frugality, in order to accumulate with a view to independence, advancement, and provision against casualities.

3. ITS SUBJECTIVE EXERCISE:

HABITS REQUISITE FOR TRAINING THE MENTAL ENDOWMENTS:

(A) *Observation*	The *fixing* of thought with a view to acquiring knowledge.
(B) *Attention*	The *fixity* of thought with a view to making progress in knowledge.
(C) *Examination*	The *scrutiny* of thought or things with a view to attaining accurate knowledge.
(D) *Application*	The *intensity* of thought with a view to attaining complete knowledge.
(E) *Study*	Application of the mind with a view to the absorption of thought.
(F) *Reflection*	Direction of the mind upon information previously absorbed.

(G) *Diligence*	A steady and constant application of our energies and powers to a selected and set purpose.
(H) *Industry*	A settled and high-principled diligence.
(I) *Sedulousness*	Industry in a particular direction that leaves little or no room for other matters.
(J) *Assiduousness*	Industry in a particular direction, as specialists. As the range of knowledge increases this quality is increasingly necessary for success.

JUSTICE

That principle which directs the rendering to every creature, idea, or thing its due right or desert the stabilizing factor in time and eternity.

A. TRUTH
Justice in precept. Exact conformity of thought, word, and deed with the real.

1. ITS SUBJECTIVE EXERCISE:
(A) *Truthfulness* — That habit or custom of the mind to choose and deal with facts in an honest manner.

2. ITS OBJECTIVE EXERCISE:
(A) *Veracity* — The true representation of things.

B. EQUITY

Rectified human justice. Human arrangements and laws on account of the rotation of circumstances continually deviate from the strict line of right and need adjustment. The wise application of law to varying human conditions.

C. RIGHTEOUSNESS

The outworking of justice in everyday dealings.

1. HONESTY: *Acting with conscious regard to justice.*
A. ITS SUBJECTIVE FIELD:

1. In regard to the habits requisite to fulfill duty:
(A) As to TIME, namely:

(a) *Diligence*	Losing no time, keeping close to work.
(b) *Promptness*	Readiness for practical purposes.
(c) *Expeditiousness*	Acting with celerity.
(d) *Punctuality*	Scrupulous regard to time.

(B) As to MANNER, namely:

(a) *Accuracy*	With regard to the care bestowed.
(b) *Correctness*	With reference to some rule or standard.

(c) *Exactness*	Without defect or redundance as compared with the original.
(d) *Precision*	Conformity with some rule or model in the mode of action.
(e) *Strictness*	Rigorously nice.
(f) *System*	Regular connection and adaptation or subordination of parts to each other, and to the design of the whole.
(g) *Order*	According to rule and in a regular and successive manner.
(h) *Method*	Acting according to a natural or convenient order.
(i) *Science*	Knowing how. Evincing profound and systematic knowledge.

2. In relation to personal character:

(A) *Rectitude*	Absolute conformity to the rule of right in principle and practice.
(B) *Uprightness*	Fulfilling obligations from right principles.
(C) *Integrity*	Fulfilling obligations from a high standard of self-respect.
(D) *Probity*	Fulfilling one's obligations from a sense of honor and duty.
(E) *Conscientiousness*	Fulfilling one's obligations according to the dictates of conscience.
(F) *Honorableness*	Action animated by a just and proper aim, or intention.

(G) *Genuineness*	Real in respect to the standard in question and noble.
(H) *Consistency*	Unchangableness of conduct in relation to principle.
(I) *Constency*	Continuity in conduct.

B. ITS OBJECTIVE FIELD:

1. As shown in dealing with others:

(A) *Faithfulness*	Fulfilling obligation; not merely to the letter but to the spirit.
(B) *Good Faith*	To act faithfully to the extent of confidence pledged or engaged.
(C) *Trustworthiness*	Proved fidelity.
(D) *Candor*	Openness of conduct under moral effort.
(E) *Frankness*	Natural openness of conduct.
(F) *Straightforwardness*	Unrestrained frankness of character.
(G) *Incorruptibility*	Proof against debasing overtures. Not to be bribed or seduced.

2. Its negative aspects:

(A) *Naturalness*	Conformity to nature, truth, or reality.
(B) *Transparency*	Using no arts to hide one's motives.
(C) *Innocence*	Freedom from guilt
(D) *Guilelessness*	Freedom from dissembling.
(E) *Simplicity*	Freedom from duplicity.

2. FAIRNESS: *Honesty in dealing.*

A. IN REGARD TO THE RIGHTS OF OTHERS:

(1) by prerogative:

(A) *Obedience*	Subject to rightful restraint or control.
(B) *Loyalty*	Obedience united to reverence or love. Truth and affection.

(2) by equality or generally:

(A) *Civility*	Avoiding to be rude.
(B) *Politeness*	Trying to please. Treating others just as you love to be treated.
(C) *Chivalry*	Homage to weakness involving courage and self-sacrifice.
(D) *Courtesy*	Elegance of manner.
(E) *Urbanity*	Polished refinement. Not cting as a rude rustic but as a cultured person.

B. IN REGARD TO THE MERITS OF OTHERS:

(A) *Respect*	Regard to rank or worth.
(B) *Reverence*	Respect, coupled with love, or fear, or esteem.
(C) *Deference*	Yielding our opinions to those of persona of acknowledged superiority.
(D) *Admiration*	Respect coupled with affection.
(E) *Veneration*	Respect for tried and matured excellence.

66

(F) *Awe*   Respect and fear at overwhelming
                             degree of superiority. Homage to
                             power and greatness.

C. IN REGARD TO THE DEMERITS OP OTHERS:
(A) *Indignation*   Revolt of feeling against injustice.
(B) *Resentment*   Feeling aroused to retaliation. A
                             weapon for defense only.

D. IN REGARD TO THE GOOD OFFICES OP OTHERS:
(A) *Gratitude*   An inner state. Thankfulness mingled
                             with affection.
(B) *Thankfulness*   An acknowledgment of favors.
                             Thanksgiving would be a more
                             accurate word.

3. IMPARTIALITY: *Honesty in dealing to the exclusion of one's personal interests, prejudices, prepossessions and bias.*

LOVE

That principle which prompts wisdom to devise ways and means, approvable by justice and performable by power, whereby good can be done to others, as well as ourselves. Well-wishing and well-doing combined.

1. GENERALLY

A. BENEVOLENCE: *well-wishing -— the least that love can do. The motive which prompts us to seek the good of others for their owns sake.*

1. INWARD CHARACTER:

(A) *Humane Feelings*	Motive power of action due to civilizing influences around us.
(B) *Kindness*	Tact. Rather a social than a moral virtue.
(C) *Loving-kindness*	An intensified kindness.
(D) *Disinterestedness*	Refers to the purity of motive, as for others, and not for our own interests.

B. BENEFICENCE: *Well-doing. Charity. Seeking the welfare of others by the exercise of our moral responsibilities.*

1. OUTWARD EXPRESSION:

(A) *Self-denial*	Giving up something for a person or a cause.
(B) *Self-devotion*	Consecration of one's self to a cause.
(C) *Self-sacrifice*	Giving up one's self to a cause regardless of consequence to the sacrificer.

2. THE DISPOSITION REQUISITE FOR DOING GOOD TO OTHERS
A. ITS INWARD EXPRESSION:

(a) *Good Will*	Being favorably disposed to help.
(b) *Good Humor*	A happy frame of mind.
(c) *Good Nature*	A readiness to oblige others.
(d) *Agreeableness*	A readiness to please others.
(e) *Amiability*	The easy manners of a character desirous of pleasing. A kind disposition.
(f) *Geniality*	Sympathetically cheerful and cheering. Pleasantness of manner.
(g) *Affability*	The easy manners of a character desirous of winning or gaining one's

end. Ready to speak with, and to be spoken to by others.

(H) *Graciousness*	The generous disposition that prompts a superior to appreciate and honor an inferior.
(I) *Benignity*	The disposition on the part of a Superior to act kindly to an 1nferior.

B. ITS OUTWARD EXPRESSION:

(A) *Obligingness*	Readiness with more than mere courtesies of demeanor; and pleasure in doing some actual service.
(B) *Accommodation*	The disposition to meet the particular or specific requirements of the time and occasion in favor of others, even at the cost of a little personal inconvenience.
(C) *Complaisance*	Desire to please, especially on the part of those who have superiority or power on their sides
(D) *Consideration*	Meeting the wants of others, or relieving them of trouble, by placing one's self thoughtfully in their place and circumstances.
(E) *Suavity*	Pleasantness of manner.
(F) *Accessibility*	Sacrifice of time, inclination, and convenience for the accommodation

of others. Readiness to receive and
hear applicants.

3. AS MANIFEST IN CONNECTION WITH THE DISTRESS OF OTHERS

A. AS TO INWARD CHARACTER:

(A) *Sympathy*	Puts one's self on a level with the sufferer. The extent of our sympathy is determined by that of our sensibility.
(B) *Compassion*	Sympathy merely on the ground of mercy.
(C) *Pity*	Sympathy, with a certain recoil of the mind toward the sufferer.
(D) *Kind-heartedness*	Readily disposed to benovelent actions.

B. AS TO OUTWARD EXPRESSION:

(A) *Liberality*	Refers to the warmth of spirit, and to largeness of giving.
(B) *Generousness*	Refers to the extent of the sacrifce made.
(C) *Munificence*	Refers to the quality and the quantity of things bestowed.

4. AS MANIFEST IN CONNECTION WITH THE FAULTS OF OTHERS

(A) *Forgiveness*	Completely dispensing with a moral account against an offender; forgetting the offense as far as any vindictive feeling or desire for further settlement is concerned.
(B) *Mercifulness*	Justice tempered by love.
(C) *Indulgence*	Yeilding freely to the wishes and feelings of those under our care.
(D) *Tenderness*	Dealing feelingly with the offender.
(E) *Clemency*	The disposition which does not enforce justice to the full against the offender.
(F) *Leniency*	Marks the character of an act which is clement.
(G) *Peacemaking*	Ardently endeavoring to rouse and to bring into play feelings of amity and concord around us.
(H) *Peaceableness*	Trying to conciliate the offender, and not insisting too strictly upon our rights and claims.
(I) *Inoffensiveness*	Not giving offense.

5. AS MANIFEST IN CONNECTION WITH THE GOOD QUALITIES OF OTHERS

(A) *Esteem*	Our appreciation of the good qualities of others.
(B) *Regard*	Approbation of the exercise of qualities of others.

6. DOING GOOD TO OTHERS RELATED TO US

A. FAMILY LOVE, as :

(a) *Paternal and Maternal*	Self-originating love springingfrom our natural relationships.
(b) *Filial*	Responsive love of children to parents.
(c) *Fraternal*	Social love of children to each other.
(d) *Conjugal*	Social and sexual love of husband and wife.

B. SOCIAL LOVE, as regards:

(a) *Friends*	Love from affinities and interest, and association.
(b) *Neighbors*	Love from convenience and interest, and acquaintance.
(c) *Citizens*	Pariotism: the having at heart and working for the good of one's countrymen. Love from a sense of common danger, from training, convenience, and a sense of duty and common interest.
(d) *Master and Servant*	Love, from respect and convenience of mutual acquaintance.

POWER

The capacity for performance, here viewed from the standpoint of the individual's subjective capacity — or self-control. Power is indispensable to the practice of either wisdom, justice, or love. Power is either latent (passive) or kinetic (active), the latter being denominated force, or applied power, and the former, might.

1. THE ENTHRONEMENT OR DETHRONEMENT OF A DESIRE OR SET OF DESIRES
A. GENERALLY :

(A) *Self-control*	The government and regulation of all our natural appetites, desires, and affections.
(B) *Self-conquest*	To have one's self in one's own power. Those who can command themselves, command others.
(C) *Temperance*	Moderation as to pleasure, generally of touch and taste.

B. AS TO THE MEANS EMPLOYED:

(A) *Decision*	Choice out of several courses after deliberation. Taking a stand, and keeping to the stand taken.
(B) *Determination*	The adhering to our choice uninfluenced by circumstances.
(C) *Resolution*	Adhering to our choice regardless of consequences.
(D) *Fixity of Purpose*	Unmovableness in the pursuit of the object of our choice
(E) *Tenacity of Purpose*	Pursuing one's course with dogged persistence in spite of all dangers and temptations.
(F) *Steadiness Stability*	Uniformity of action or principle. in pursuit of one's choice.
(G) *Unchangeableness*	Habit of mind leading to steadiness.

2. ENLISTING EMOTION

(A) *Energy*   Power efficiently exerted in one's self.

(B) *Enthusiasm*   Aspiration inspired by firm belief in the ideal perfection of one's cause.

(C) *Zeal*   Fired energy.

(D) *Earnestness*   Intensity of desire, with a sense of the gravity of the cause.

(E) *Ardor*   Concentration of Energy until it is wrought up to a high heat.

(F) *Fervor*   With not quite as intense but steadier flame than that of ardor.

3. CONTROL OF THE BODILY APPETITES

(A) *Temperance*	Regulated indulgence as to eating and drinking.
(B) *Abstemiousness*	Restricted eating and drinking on account of special circumstances.
(C) *Sobriety*	Freedom from Intoxication — keeping one's balance.
(D) *Moderation*	Imposing due restraint upon our appetites.
(E) *Chastity*	Imposing due restraint upon sex desire.
(F) *Continence*	Restraining conjugal indulgence within ties.
(G) *Purity*	Chastity with reference more to the mind.
(H) *Cleanliness*	The removal of any element of impurity by which either body or mind is disfigured or dishonored.

4. CONTROL OF THE EMOTION OF FEAR

(A) *Boldness*	Meeting danger, defensive attitude.
(B) *Daring*	Courting danger, offensive attitude.
(C) *Bravery*	Laudable contest with danger and difficulties.
(D) *Resolution*	Having a purpose and sticking to it.
(E) *Enterprise*	Promptness to undertake and seek spheres of action.
(F) *Valor*	Bravery in war.
(G) *Undauntedness*	Awed by nothing but sin and wrong-doing.
(H) *Intrepidity*	A firm, unshaken confidence without fear or trepidation.
(I) *Fortitude*	Endurance with perseverance.
(J) *Heroism*	The genius of courage.

5. REGULATION AND HEALTHY DEVELOPMENT OF HOPE

A. AS TO ITS ACTIVE SIDE:

(A) *Cheerfulness*	A disposition to discern and enjoy the bright side of things and not to take too gloomy a view of one's fortune.
(B) *Hopefulness*	A disposition to rise above the depressing effect of present circumstances by consideration of the probably brighter future.

B. AS TO ITS PASSIVE SIDE:

(A) *Endurance*	Carrying the load uphill and to the very summit without fainting.
(B) *Confidence*	Freedom from doubts. Having faith in success.
(C) *Reliance*	Trusting to the efficiency and sufficiency of the means employed to secure the end.
(D) *Self-reliance*	Trusting to one's own powers and resources as sufficient to the end.
(E) *Calmness*	Freedom from agitation.
(F) *Collectedness*	A quality requisite for determined promptitude. Calmness in a storm.
(G) *Composedness*	Calmness *after* a storm.

6. CONTROL OF THE EMOTION OF PRIDE
A. ITS PASSIVE SIDE:

(A) *Humility*	A willingness to occupy one's appropriate sphere in respect to God and his providences.
(B) *Lowliness*	The spirit in which humility is exercised.
(C) *Diffidence*	Distrust in our own powers.
(D) *Tractableness*	Easily managed or taught. Willing to be guided.
(E) *Modesty*	Absence of all overconfidence and conceit.
(F) *Docility*	A consciousness of our own ignorance, and a childlike readiness.

B. ITS ACTIVE SIDE:

(A) *Independence*	Self-respect in directing ones own affairs, without being burdensome to others, and resenting improper interference.
(B) *Nobleness*	Elevation of mind above what is low, mean, degrading, dishonorable.
(C) *Magnanimity*	Sacrificing one's feelings and interests, or yielding one's claims for the accomplishment of some noble object.

7. CONTROL OF THE ANIMAL SPIRITS

(A) *Soberness*	Opposed to the extravagant in thought or action.
(B) *Quietness*	Opposed to nervousness and restlessness.
(C) *Sedateness*	Opposed to the undignified and unbecoming.
(D) *Tranquility*	Freedom from agitation.
(E) *Staidness*	Opposed to the frivalous.
(F) *Seriousness*	Opposed to the jocose.
(G) *Solemnity*	Opposed to unseemly ebullition of mirth and to irreverence.
(H) *Gravity*	Opposed to the levitous.
(I) *Serenity*	Tranquility of the highest order; might be ranked as the reflex influence of wisdom.
(J) *Modesty and Reserve*	Womanly adjuncts to virtue.

8. RIGHT DEVELOPMENT OF TASTE, CHIEFLY
A. IN REGARD TO DEALING WITH THINGS:

(A) *Tidiness*	Having things in good order.
(B) *Neatness*	Having things free from that which spoils their beauty or effect. Cleanliness or tidiness with a view to effect.
(C) *Trimness*	Having things in a certain shapely and elegant firmness.

B. IN REGARD TO CONDUCT:

(A) *Decency*	That which is becoming in conduct.
(B) *Decorum*	That which is becoming in behavior.
(C) *Propriety*	Consonance with established principles, rules, or customs.
(D) *Seemliness*	Decency in minor morals.
(E) *Fitness*	Regulated by local circumstances.
(F) *Suitableness*	With reference to the person, occasion, etc.
(G) *Becoming*	That which presents a pleasant exterior.

9. CONTROL OF PASSIONS OPPOSED TO LOVE

(A) *Gentleness*	Acting without offending.
(B) *Meekness*	Forbearing under Injuries; also the disposition which delights in exercising forbearance and gentleness.
(C) *Mildness*	An absence of all that is acrid, harsh, or discordant in action.
(D) *Tolerance*	Regard for the *opinions* of others; or, more accurately, regard for the right of others, humanly considered, to hold such.
(E) *Indulgence*	Touching the *faults* of others.
(F) *Long-suffering*	In regard to the *trespasses* of others.
(G) *Forbearance*	As regards the trespasses of others, only under certain conditions.

10. CONTROL OF THE TEMPER, CHIEFLY

(A) *Uncomplaining*	The negatire side of patience.
(B) *Patience*	Carrying the load of cares without irritation.
(C) *Contentment*	The acquiescence of the mind in the portion of good which we possess. Absence of restlessness and timidity.
(D) *Satisfaction*	The desire fulfilled.
(E) *Resignation*	The submission of the will to a superior, acknowledging both his power and right to afflict.
(F) *Submission*	Bowing to the will of a superior, with unresisting, unmurmuring acquiescence.

Fredrik Homer Robison
February 3, 1885 -- April 17, 1932

The only son of schoolteacher James A. Robison[1] and Eva J. Robison[2] grew up in Greenwood, Indiana. It is said that he graduated from high school at the age of fourteen. He was the middle child of a family of five, which included two sisters; Bertha B. (born 6/1883) and May E. (born 5/1889).

It was during his mid-teen years that religion became his most serious interest and he decided to affiliate with the Disciples of Christ. Feeling called to the Ministry, he enrolled at Franklin College to continue his education in those subjects he felt would be most beneficial to his future path.

In approximately 1903 he left Indiana for Canada where he took out a claim in the Rainy River district of Ontario, and taught part time and also worked part time for the immigration service. He returned to Indiana in 1904, entered Butler College in Indianapolis as a sophomore and remained there one year. He then enrolled in the Winona Technical Institute in Indianapolis, where he familiarized himself with the lithographer's craft, thinking that a trade would be useful to him in his planned missionary work. At this time he thought that he would carry the gospel to Japan.

While working as a foreman in a lithography house in Cleveland Ohio he first read Pastor Russell's STUDIES IN THE SCRIPTURES, and convinced a Japanese friend to translate some of the literature into Japanese, still thinking of foreign mission work, a plan that he later abandoned to become a colporteur for Pastor Russell's Watch Tower Society.

---

[1] born. 11/1859 Indiana; died 24 Mar 1949

[2] nee Whitenack, born Apr. 1862 Indiana; married. 27 Apr 1881; died Feb.1955

After one year as a colporteur he was invited to the headquarters of the Watch Tower Bible and Tract Society, in Allegheny, Pennsylvania. There he met Minnie Almeta Nation[3], who he married in 1909. He became private secretary to Pastor Russell and held that position until after the Society's offices were transferred to Brooklyn, New York in 1909, when he became secretary in charge of the foreign work. In the pages of The Watch Tower he is often referred to as "Professor" Robison, though no explanation of his academic credentials is offered.

As secretary of the foreign work he had the opportunity to pursue the study of languages and it is said that he could translate twenty-three languages in all, giving discourses in German, Greek, and English. He made week-end pilgrimages in and about New York City, addressing both public and private gatherings.

Pastor Russell, London and
Brooklyn Tabernacles,
Chairman I. B. S. A.
Committee.

General Wm. P. Hall,
U. S. A., Washington, D. C.
I. B. S. A. Committee.

Prof. F. H. Robison, Linguist,
Secretary I. B. S. A.
Committee.

The Watch Tower, January 1, 1912

F. H. Robison was one of four men designated in the 1907 will of Pastor Russell to be co-editors of the Watch Tower magazine, the official organ of the Watch Tower Bible and Tract Society. Robison's wife was one of the three women who signed as witnesses of Pastor Russell's Will & Testament. In 1918, F. H. Robison was one of

---

[3](b. Nov. 1878, d. Jan. 25, 1958)

the officers of the Watch Tower Society who was charged with sedition and sentenced to 80 years in Federal prison[4].

When the Society's printing plates for the Emphatic Diaglott translation of the Bible became worn out, the Watch Tower Society looked for another translation. In late 1919/early 1920 Robison was delegated to call on Mr. Adolph Ernst Knoch of the Concordant Publishing Concern in Los Angeles, with a view to putting the Concordant Version on the Society's list of literature. When Robison arrived he was told that the Concordant Version could not, in any way, be changed to suit the views of the Watch Tower Society. Robison responded, "That is just what we want!" An agreement was made that the Society would buy 10,000 copies of the Concordant Version. It was advertised in the June 15, 1920 issue of The Watch Tower as the "popular edition, without notes." This was no small advertisement: it filled one and one third pages of the magazine.

Robison enjoyed his theological discussions with A. E. Knoch. As he became more interested in the doctrines of Christian Universalism[5], Robison's position in the Watch Tower Society became precarious.

In the spring of 1922 F. H. Robison resigned as co-editor of the Watch Tower and elder of the New York congregation. In response to the many inquiries as to why he left the Society, he published an explanation.

---

[4]Those were: Joseph F. Rutherford, President; William E. Van Amburgh, Secretary-Treasurer; Robert J. Martin, office manager; Frederick H. Robison, a member of the editorial committee for The Watch Tower; A. Hugh Macmillan, a director of the Society; George H. Fisher and Clayton J. Woodworth, compilers of The Finished Mystery.

[5]The belief that *everything* in heaven and on earth will ultimately be reconciled back to the Creator through the work of Jesus Christ, his Son. Also known as "Universal Reconciliation."

The last mention of his name is in the masthead of the April 15, 1922 Watchtower; it was replaced in the May 1, 1922 issue by J. Hemery.

Additional high ranking Bible Students accepted the teachings of Christian Universalism: Walter H. Bundy, Menta Sturgeon, O.L. Sullivan, W.T. Hooper, C.B. Shull, J.O. Mellinder, Axel Sjo, and a majority of Bible Students in Sweden and Finland.

An interesting sidenote: In November of 1927 J. F. Rutherford sent the following letter to the publisher of the Concordant Version:

WATCH TOWER BIBLE & TRACT SOCIETY
PRESIDENT'S OFFICE
124 COLUMBIA HEIGHTS, BROOKLYN, N.Y., U.S.A.

Nov. 25th, 1927.

The Concordant Publishing Concern,
2823 E. 6th St., Los Angeles, Calif.

Dear Sirs:

A copy of a booklet issued by you has been received. On page 327 you speak of a grievance against the International Bible Students Association. As you well know the Society is a corporation. The notice was inserted in the WATCH TOWER by one who had no authority. The order was given by one who had no authority to order them. When I found that you were advocating universal salvation including the Devil himself, I took steps to see that our Society had nothing whatsoever to do with the distribution of the Concordant Version, and that was the first time it was called to my attention as to how the notice got in the WATCH TOWER.

In the service of the Redeemer,
J. F. RUTHERFORD

Yet the "popular edition" of the Concordant Version that the Watchtower was selling had no notes by the translator, or any indications of his doctrinal views on any subject just as requested by the Robison during his initial visit some seven years earlier. During those years the Watchtower had only sold 2,000 copies of the Concordant Version. Was Rutherford seeking an easy way out of the agreement, or was he "punishing" A. E. Knoch for the conversion of Robison and so many others?

In response to Rutherford's cancellation of the order, Knoch wrote in reply,

Dear Sir:

I wish to thank you for your letter assuring me that the notice of the CONCORDANT VERSION in THE WATCH TOWER of June 15, 1920 was inserted without authority. I am sorry that you find it necessary to offer an excuse which so sorely lacks the support of the facts, which are as follows:

A number of members of the Society who had seen the CONCORDANT VERSION were so pleased with it that they wrote to headquarters. I never approached the Society at all. They wrote to me on their official stationery, signed by a name recognized in THE WATCH TOWER. One of the editors was sent to see me. I told him that I did not agree with some of the doctrines of the International Bible Students Association, and that this was to be distinctly understood, so that they could not repudiate any agreement on the ground of differences in doctrine. To this he heartily agreed. I had assured myself of his identity by going to an International Bible Students Association conference and found that he was a recognized national leader. Because the regular edition contained my notes, it was agreed that I print a special edition for your use, without any notes whatever.

In THE WATCH TOWER I found this notice: "This Journal is published under the supervision of an Editorial Committee, at least three of whom must have read and have approved as Truth each and every article appearing in these columns. The names of the Editorial Committee now serving are: W. E. VAN AMBURGH, J. F. RUTHERFORD, H. C. ROCKWELL, F. H. ROBINSON, R. H. HIRCH."

I know of no other publication which is so thoroughly safeguarded against unofficial announcements. This is more than sufficient evidence that the commendation of the Version was not inserted by one who had no right to do so, but was backed by the authority of the leaders and published as the official voice of the Society. You asked me if I had a written contract. The endorsement of the Society was a {printed} contract, not only with me but with your members, and {it was my bounded duty to do my part in fulfilling it}. You sold about two thousand parts and paid for them with checks signed by your treasurer. He certainly had authority, for the cheeks were all honored.

Then, notwithstanding the verbal agreement, which is just as binding on saints as a written document, notwithstanding the printed advertisement guaranteed by your editorial committee, and after you had sold and paid for thousands of copies, without a moment's warning you repudiated your word and your public announcement {on grounds which it was expressly agreed should not affect our business relations on any account}.

You are forced to use versions made by men who do not fully agree with your doctrinal position. There are no others. The CONCORDANT VERSION is the only one which has a practical plan to exclude the private opinion of the translator. No one who renders each Greek word consistently {can} introduce his own ideas, as is done in the Emphatic Diaglott on almost every opening. Without special examination, I have noticed the same Greek word translated four different ways on a single page. {Your reason for rejecting the CONCORDANT VERSION is the very one which should force you to accept it}. It alone, of all versions, has on elaborate plan which makes a deliberate effort to exclude private interpretation, and it alone will provide its readers with the evidence to test each rendering.

I believe that God "through the Son of His love" will "reconcile all things for Him, having made peace by means of the blood of His cross, whether the things on the earth, or the things in the heavens" (Col.1:20, Emphatic Diaglott). You do not believe this. I do. This is my crime.

Your own friends here who knew about your course did what they could to get you to right the wrong. They arranged a meeting at which I asked you to make some announcement in THE WATCH TOWER. You refused to give any reason for your action or to do anything, because I had no written contract. Being a lawyer, you knew better than I that we had much more than that. I confess that such an attitude from one in your position, under the circumstances, was exceedingly painful to me. I suppose men of the world will go back on their word under the plea of a written contract, but I hoped that you were actuated by superior principles.

I am sorry to see that your letter shows the same spirit. You say the Society is a corporation. I have heard of soulless corporations which descended to anything legal to gain their ends, even repudiating the acts of their employees. Surely you do not voluntarily class your Society among these! Your friends, of course, are responsible with you, but I do not hold it against them, because everyone of them who hears of it is shocked by your attitude.

Lastly, the "Popular" versions, specially prepared for you, had absolutely no indication of our teaching whatever. The Emphatic Diaglott, which you publish, has very much to indicate the bias of the author in its text and notes, yet Pastor Russell contented himself with calling attention to such differences.

I need say no more. You do not seek to justify your action, but prefer to introduce legal technicalities, such as "a written contract" and "a corporation." Does not this convince you, as it does all others, that all is not right in the sight of God?

Yours in the Lord,
A. E. KNOCH

Robison left the Brooklyn headquarters of the Watch Tower and went to Washington, D. C., to work in the art department of the Washington Post. After that he worked for the government and still later became art director for the American Automobile Association headquarters in Washington, D. C..

Robison conducted an independent Bible study class in Washington, D. C., and also served on the faculty of the Columbia Bible Training School, conducting studies in the life and epistles of Saint Paul until he returned to New York to look for a job in the fall of 1931. He contracted a serious cold, and because no one in his office understood his job well enough to take over for him, he forced himself out of his sickbed, returning to work sooner than he should have. This cost him his life.

Robison developed pneumonia and pleurisy, and after six days and nights of suffering, died at age 47. A funeral service was held that same day. The next day his body was shipped to Greenwood Cemetery in Indianapolis accompanied by his wife.

After services he was buried in a most beautiful spot, with the birds he loved so much singing overhead, not far from where he and his sisters used to play.

Photo courtesy of J. Pierle

The Message of the Hour

Millions Now Living will Never Die !

You may be one of them !

Do these things appeal to you? Unending human life; perpetual health; lasting and satisfying political adjustments; comprehensive economic arrangements; no more fear of the landlord, the doctor, the sheriff, the employer, of evil men and angels, of vicious animals, of dependent old age; no more blindness, lameness, deafness, dumbness; no more bald heads, glass eyes, false teeth, or wooden legs; no more sickness, disease, or pestilence; no more ignorance or superstition; no more sorrow; no more tears!

No, we are not trifling: these things and more are absolutely sure, because promised by the Word of God. The world has already ended, in the Bible and only proper sense of that term; and the antitypical Jubilee, earth's times of restitution, its springtime, begins to count in 1926.

When that time comes, all the above blessings will not come instantaneously, but will come *speedily* on those who live through the next five or six years of trouble. Suppose nine of every ten people now living on earth should die of famine, pestilence, customary disease, and violence during the next five years (surely a much too extreme estimate), there would still be living 160,000,000 people to be the first human beneficiaries of the promise of Jesus: "Whosoever liveth and believeth on me, shall never die". — John 11:26.

This topic, in lecture form, has been recently treated by Judge Rutherford before gatherings in most of the large cities of the United States, Great Britain, Continental Europe, Egypt & Palestine. The attendances have been phenomenal and the interest profound.

Because of this great interest, and in response to repeated requests to have the lecture in print, Judge Rutherford has arranged it in amplified form, with elaborate substantiation, both from Scripture and from current events.

Now obtainable as a neatly bound, high quality replica reprint !

From your bookseller or on the internet.
ISBN 1-4116-2898-5

SENDING THE IDEA HOME

Millions now living will never die

In the world is a class of individuals who have what a bishop has aptly named the "ecclesiastical mind." Its chief characteristic is that it has become ossified, which means that the skull is practically impregnable to a new thought. As the creeds are inflexible and not permitted to advance with civilization, those who are creed-bound are in the dark and exceedingly loath to depart from traditions. But the light will break through—eventually.

(from The GOLDEN AGE, March 14, 1923 page 6 .)